NEW ORLEANS

THE GROWTH OF THE CITY

NEW ORLEANS

THE GROWTH OF THE CITY

Steve Bryant

CHARTWELL
BOOKS, INC.

This edition published in 2007 by

CHARTWELL BOOKS, INC.
A Division of
BOOK SALES, INC.
114 Northfield Avenue
Edison, New Jersey 08837

ISBN-13: 978-0-7858-2211-0
ISBN-10: 0-7858-2211-9

© 2007 Compendium Publishing, 43 Frith Street, London,
Soho, W1V 4SA, United Kingdom

Cataloging-in-Publication data is available from the Library
of Congress

Printed and bound in China

Design: Ian Hughes/Compendium Design

Page 2: The statue of General Andrew Jackson on his horse in front of the St.
Louis Cathedral in New Orleans. The general led an army of pirates, French
landowners, free African-Americans, and frontiersmen to victory against a
British invasion of New Orleans in 1815.

Page 4: The intricate cast- and wrought-iron balconies of the French Quarter
and Garden District are an integral part of New Orleans' unique character.

Contents

Introduction

A view of New Orleans, from Algiers Point, showing a large, modern city on the banks of the river that has been so integral to its development.

Introduction

The city of New Orleans has a captivating and colorful history. One of the top tourist destinations in the United States, it is renowned worldwide as a party town where the residents are always ready to "laissez les bons temps rouler" (let the good times roll). When most people think of New Orleans they think of the wild abandon of Mardi Gras and the vibrant sounds of jazz music, but it is also a city of indomitable character that has had to display great spirit in the face of seemingly insurmountable odds throughout its history.

From the outset, New Orleans was to be both blighted and blessed by its location; the urban geographer Pierce F. Lewis once described it as "an inevitable city on an impossible site," and a cursory glance at a map of North America is enough to reveal the reasons for his description. Stretching from the Great Lakes to the Gulf of Mexico, from the Rocky Mountains to the Appalachians, the Mississippi and its huge network of tributaries provides a readymade system for the transportation of people and cargo across the vast mid-continent of North America. A city located at the ocean mouth of such an excellent natural network was indeed inevitable. Such a prime geographical location would come at a cost though, Lewis's description of the site as "impossible" rings true because from the outset the inhabitants of the Crescent City had to cope with hurricanes,

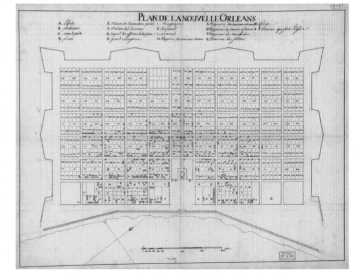

floods, fire, and mosquito-born epidemics of both yellow fever and malaria.

Prior to the arrival of European explorers in the area, it was inhabited by Native-Americans who lived in the area around Bayou St. John, known to them as *Bayouk Choupique*. The first European to discover the Mississippi River was the Spanish explorer Hernando de Soto in 1541, but it took until 1682 for a European nation to stake a claim for the land around modern-day New Orleans. Rather than the Spanish it was a Frenchman, Robert de La Salle, who sailed down the Mississippi in that year and

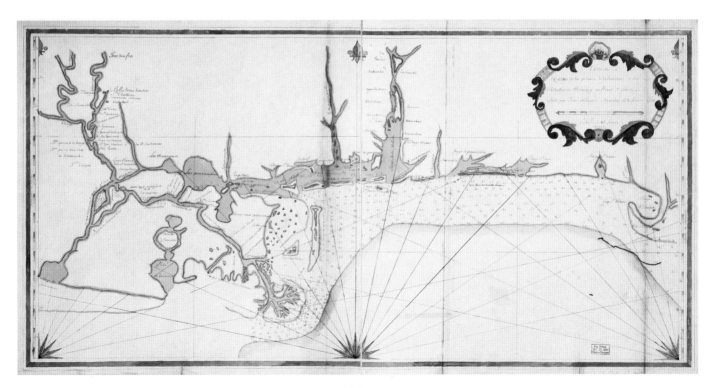

A view of the New Orleans riverfront busy with sailing ships during the 1840s; these were the boom times for New Orleans when the river trade was bringing enormous wealth into the city.

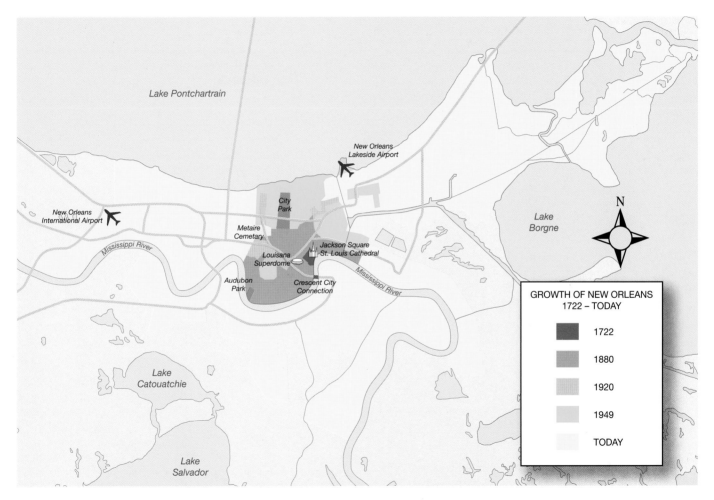

Lake Pontchartrain

New Orleans
Lakeside Airport

New Orleans
International Airport

City
Park

Metaire
Cemetery

Louisana
Superdome

Jackson Square
St. Louis Cathedral

Audubon
Park

Crescent City
Connection

Mississippi River

Mississippi River

Lake
Borgne

N

Lake
Catouatchie

Lake
Salvador

GROWTH OF NEW ORLEANS
1722 – TODAY

	1722
	1880
	1920
	1949
	TODAY

planted a cross to claim the area that would become Louisiana for the French monarch, King Louis XIV.

The first French settlers began to arrive during the 1690s, mainly fur trappers and traders. By 1701, an encampment called Port Bayou St. Jean had been established and was guarded by a small fort—"St. Jean," located at the mouth of the bayou.

In 1718, the French-Canadian naval officer, Jean-Baptiste Le Moyne, Sieur de Bieneville, founded the town of Nouvelle-Orleans and three years later the engineer Adrien de Pauger set out what is now the French Quarter in a series of military style grids with the Place d'Armes (now Jackson Square) military parade ground occupying the center portion of the town, facing the levee. Nouvelle-Orleans was named in honor of Philip II, Duke of Orleans, who was at the time regent of France. Many of the streets that are now synonymous with New Orleans still retain their original names. Chartres, Bourbon, Burgundy, Conti, and Toulouse streets were all named for sons or sons-in-law of King Louis XIV. The Old Ursuline Convent on Chartres and Ursulines streets, built in 1745, is thought to be the oldest building in the Mississippi Valley.

Although initially enthusiastic about their American colonies, the French interest began to wane as political focus shifted to the wars in Europe. The Seven Years' war ended in 1763 with the Treaty of Paris under which Louis XV ceded Louisiana to his cousin, the Spanish King Charles III. The French settlers were furious at the idea of Spanish rule and when, in 1766, the first Spanish governor, Don Antonio de Ulloa, arrived they staged a rebellion that forced him back to Havana. The Spanish responded by sending Alexander O'Reilly, an Irish-born Spanish general, to quell the uprising. O'Reilly soon achieved his goal and on October 25, 1769, he executed six of the rebellion's ringleaders, thus bringing the uprising to an end and decisively establishing Spanish rule in Louisiana.

By relaxing strict trading restrictions that had previously hampered the growth of the city, the Spanish began to bring greater prosperity to New Orleans, though a fire in 1788 threatened the new expansion, destroying 856 buildings. Following this the Spanish ruled that all buildings over two stories were to be built of brick rather than the wood that had been prevalent previously. This decree led to both safer, more solid construction and the new buildings gave the city a more Mediterranean feel.

In the 1790s New Orleans flourished under Baron Carondelet (1792–1797), who granted free trade to the Americans on the Mississippi and opened the Carondelet Canal that connected the back of the city with Lake Pontchartrain. Both of these measures were a huge boost to commerce in the area. During this thriving time the city's first newspaper, *Le Moniteur de la Louisiane*, began publication and the first theater was opened. Drainage ditches were dug to protect the city from flooding, gas lamps began to light the streets at night, and a rudimentary police force was established.

RIGHT: An 1850s map showing the route of the New Orleans, Opelousas & Great Western Rail Road drawn by the chief engineer, G. W. R. Bayley. The first fifty miles of the railroad was opened on March 6, 1854 and its expansion helped to further New Orleans' position as the hub of Southern trade.

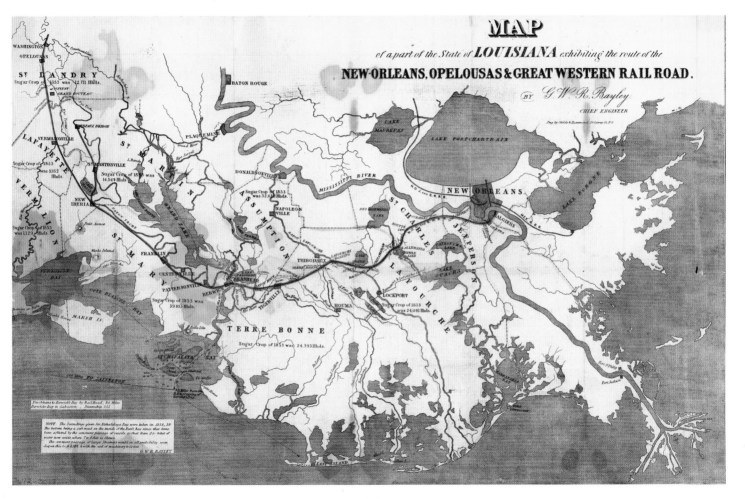

Much of the eighteenth century architecture that can still be seen in the French Quarter is from this period. Three of New Orleans most famous buildings, St. Louis Cathedral, the Cabildo, and the Presbytere, all situated in Jackson Square, were also built at this time.

In 1800, France regained control of Louisiana under the terms of the secret Treaty of Ildefonso, though far from being enthusiastic about the return, the French showed even less interest in their American colony than they had previously. Indeed, Louisiana stayed under Spanish administration until March 1803, when Pierre Clement de Laussat arrived to formally take control for France. Just one month later, Napoleon had sold Louisiana to the United States for $15,000,000. At that time the state included portions of more than a dozen present-day states and the deal worked out at around a bargain four cents an acre. General James Wilkinson and William C.C. Claiborne officially ratified the Louisiana Purchase on December 20, 1803, in the elegant salon of the Cabildo. The population of New Orleans at this time was around 10,000 people.

The following years saw the beginning of self-government for both city and state. New Orleans had already seen an influx of immigrants, fleeing the slave uprising in Haiti in 1791 and over the coming years these new citizens would be joined by refugee planters and slaves who poured into the city, helping to create the cosmopolitan population that has since made the rich atmosphere of New Orleans so unique and continues to distinguish the metropolis today. By 1812, the population of New

Two images, one a satellite view and the other a view along the Mississippi with the high-rise buildings of New Orleans Central Business District easily visible just past the bend in the river. Both demonstrate how the unpromising marshy swampland has been developed into a successful, expanding, industrial city.

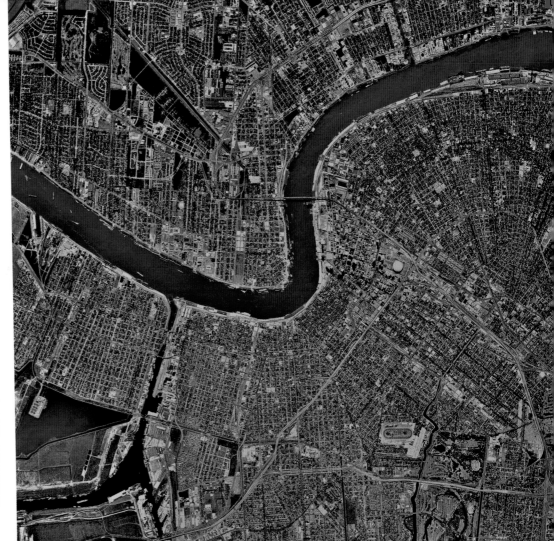

Orleans had risen to over 40,000 and tension between French Creoles and Americans had begun to escalate. This gave rise to two distinct districts—the French Quarter and an uptown American borough; Canal Street divided the areas and was the neutral ground. On April 30, in the same year, Louisiana was admitted to the Union, just six weeks before the beginning of the 1812 War. In January 1815, the last action of the war was fought when General Andrew Jackson led a mixed force of militia and regular forces to victory over the British in the Battle of New Orleans.

The arrival of the first steamboat in New Orleans (again in 1812) marked another turning point for the city, speeding up trade routes to the inland plantations and the heart of America. These were boom times for the city and the population doubled during the 1830s. By 1840 it had surpassed 102,000; New Orleans had become the fourth largest city in the United States and the largest in the South. The huge wealth being generated led to further expansion of the city—in 1852 the city of Lafayette (now the Garden District) was annexed. All of this occurred in spite of frequent outbreaks of yellow fever, the worst of which killed over 10,000 people in 1853.

Although the city itself did not suffer the destruction that blighted so many others during the American Civil War, New Orleans was nevertheless greatly affected by the conflict. By the end of the war many of the plantations that had provided the backbone of the city's booming economy had been destroyed and New Orleans struggled to recover. Despite these hard times the city continued to expand both across the river (in 1870 the city of Algiers was annexed) and up river, annexing the town of Carrolton in 1874. The population also grew as Irish and Italian immigrants flocked to the city in the latter half of the nineteenth century (legend has it that the American Mafia has its roots in New Orleans). In 1884, the city hosted the World's Industrial and Cotton Centennial Exposition, which raised the city's worldwide profile and helped boost civic morale.

With the discovery of oil beneath the Gulf of Mexico in 1901, some economic prosperity returned. Over the next twenty years refineries sprang up along the Mississippi between Baton Rouge and New Orleans. In fact, oil is still the major industry in town. However, like so many American towns and cities, New Orleans' suffered during the Great Depression, though by 1933 Mayor Robert Maestri began using money from the New Deal to regenerate New Orleans, building parks, roads, bridges, and municipal buildings. World War II saw business return to the shipyards. Thousands of the Higgins boats used during D-Day were manufactured in New Orleans (as is commemorated at the National D-Day Museum, built in 2000, on Magazine Street and Howard Avenue). Further rebuilding was undertaken under Mayor de Lesseps Story Morrison in the decades following World War II, when the city began to take on its modern appearance. A new airport, the Potchartrain Expressway, and the $65,000,000 Mississippi Bridge were constructed between 1946 and 1961.

LEFT: This night-time view shows a city skyline full of modern skyscrapers, a far cry from the hunters' huts and Indian villages that were the sole structures along the riverside only two hundred and fifty years ago.

New Orleans is fortunate in having preserved much of its early heritage and architecture—especially in the French Quarter (shown here) and Garden District. This, along with its sophisticated, cosmopolitan atmosphere made the city a prime tourist destination after World War II.

The economy was given a further boost when NASA took over the Michoud aircraft plant in the 1960s to build the Saturn rocket booster. The following years would see the construction of new skyscrapers such as the World Trade Center and One Shell Square while large hotels began to appear on Canal Street. The city benefited greatly from the oil boom of the early 1980s, but by 1986 international oil prices were dropping and the inner city began to stagnate. In an effort to counteract this the waterfront was developed and investment in tourism was actively encouraged. While this strategy was undoubtedly effective, New Orleans remains hugely dependent on the oil and tourism industries, though the introduction of some newer industries allied to the technology boom in the latter half of the 1990s helped to restore a degree of economic stability.

On August 29, 2005, disaster struck New Orleans when Hurricane Katrina made landfall on the Gulf Coast near the city. The damage caused by wind and rain was severe, but even more devastating was the destruction caused when levees failed and entire neighborhoods of New Orleans were flooded with water. The magnitude of the disaster caused repercussions throughout the United States economy and political landscape as well as touching the lives of millions of Americans. New Orleans will continue to feel the effects of this tragedy for decades to come.

LEFT: A flooded cemetery, with the city skyline in the background, a week after Hurricane Katrina battered the city. The destruction caused by the worst hurricane ever to hit New Orleans will take decades to recover from.

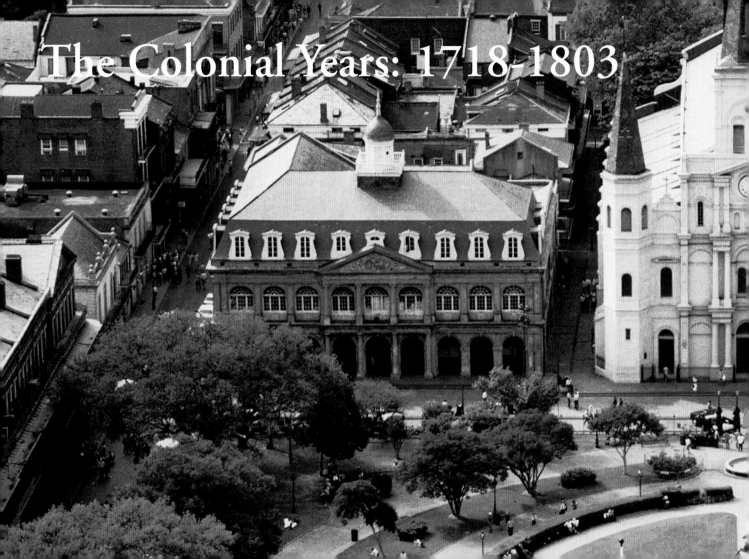

The Colonial Years: 1718-1803

The Colonial Years: 1718–1803

On arriving at the site of the recently founded Nouvelle-Orleans in January 1722, the priest-chronicler Pierre Francois Xavier de Charlevoix found the settlement to consist of nothing more than "a hundred or so shacks;" nonetheless he did concede that it could one day become "an opulent city." The first step in this direction was made in 1722 when Nouvelle-Orleans replaced Biloxi as the capital of French Louisiana. Despite this, the colony did not thrive and the French king put its fate in the hands of the Scottish entrepreneur and private financier, John Law. Law's extravagant, not to say false, advertisements for the utopia to be found in Louisiana began to lure eager settlers from Europe.

By 1731 though Law's Company of the West had gone bust and the king sent the city's original founder, Bienville, back to resume control of the colony. In spite of the strict trade restrictions the French imposed, river traffic began to increase and by the time they ceded the colony to Spain in 1763 the annual trade from the export of indigo, rum, furs, and sugar was worth over $300,000.

The fortunes of the city improved rapidly under Spanish rule, despite its unpopularity with the French inhabitants. Spain's influence in the area was increased during the American Revolution (1775–83) when the governor, Bernardo de Galvez, supporting the Americans, captured Baton Rouge, Natchez, Mobile, and Pensacola for the Spanish crown.

PREVIOUS PAGE: A modern, aerial view of Jackson Square in the heart of the French Quarter, featuring the three most important religious and administrative buildings of the city's colonial past; from left to right, the Cabildo, St. Louis Cathedral, and the Presbytere.

LEFT AND FAR LEFT: Taken from the 1920 book *The Story of Our Country* by E. Boyd Smith and an earlier engraving, these two pictures show Robert de La Salle traveling down the Mississippi in 1682 and planting a cross to claim Louisiana for the French king.

The last twenty years of the eighteenth century were marked by the continuing growth of commerce on the Mississippi and the increasing importance of New Orleans as an international trade port. In 1794–95 the failure of his indigo crop led Jean Etienne Bore to plant sugar cane. He then developed the process for making granulated sugar from his crops. The commercial production of sugar cane was to become hugely significant in the future growth of New Orleans and by the time

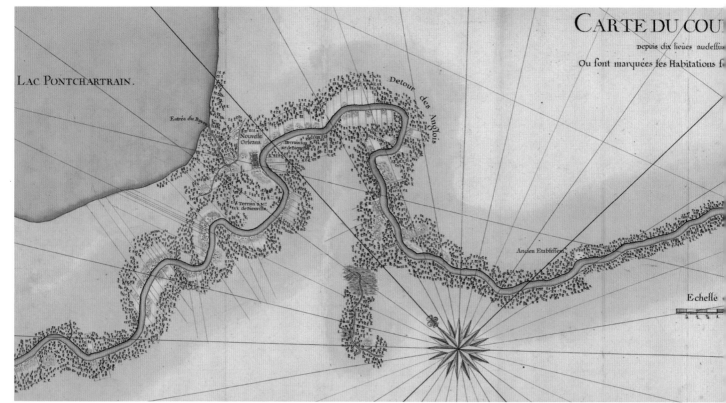

LAC PONTCHARTRAIN.

Entrée du B...

Nouvelle Orleans.

Terrain ...

Detour des Anglois

CARTE DU COU...

Depuis dix lieues audessu...

Ou sont marquées les Habitations f...

Terrain ... de Bienville.

Ancien Etablissem...

Echelle

Napoleon had regained and then sold control of Louisiana, Charlevoix's prediction of "an opulent city" was beginning to become reality.

BELOW: This map from the early 1730s shows the lower Mississippi River from the vicinity of New Orleans (Nouvelle-Orleans) to its mouth in the Gulf of Mexico. As well as the nascent city of Nouvelle-Orleans, smaller settlements can be seen dotted along the banks of the Mississippi in the surrounding area.

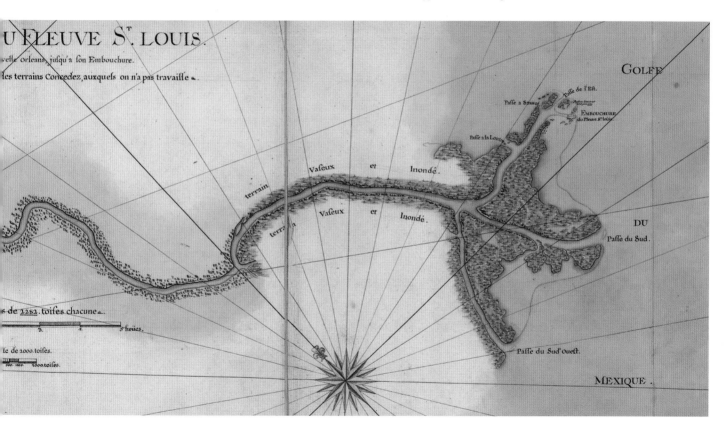

Two views of the Old Ursuline Convent on Chartres Street, one from circa 1900 and the more recent taken in 1995. Thought to be the oldest building in the Mississippi Valley, the convent was designed in 1745 and completed in 1752. It is one of the few remaining buildings from the French Colonial period. In 1788, the great fire that destroyed 856 homes in the city also threatened the convent, but Pere Antoine, aided by a "bucket brigade," saved not only this building, but also the Royal Hospital and the adjoining barracks.

Constructed during the first French period of control (the precise date is unknown) Lafitte's blacksmith shop is a good example of brick, between-posts, French-style construction. Although named after the famous pirate brothers, Jean and Pierre Lafitte, there is no proof that they ever owned or occupied the building. In recent times Lafitte's has become one of the most famous of the many bars that throng Bourbon Street.

LEFT: Currently housing the Historic New Orleans Collection, this building at 533 Royal Street was originally built in 1792 for the French merchant Jean-Francois Merieult. It was the only building in the area that was left standing after a fire in 1794 that destroyed 212 buildings.

RIGHT: Financed by Don Andres Almonester y Rojas and designed by Guilberto Guillemard, the Cabildo was built in 1795 to house the legislative assembly of the colonial Spanish government. The walls were constructed of brick with shell lime being used for the mortar. Originally the Cabildo was two stories high, with a flat roof; the Mansard roof was added in 1851. At the same time the open arches of the second storey loggia were closed, that there might be more room for offices. Between 1853 and 1911 it housed the state Supreme Court, since then it has been part of the Louisiana State Museum.

Further Adventures of the Mask

Return to New Orleans

LEFT: Reflecting the city's French heritage, one of the most legendary artifacts on display in the Cabildo is a death mask of Napoleon Bonaparte. During the chaos of the Civil War, the mask disappeared, but it eventually returned to New Orleans in 1909, since when it has again resided in the Cabildo.

FAR LEFT: An interior view of St. Louis Cathedral. The baroque altars seen at the far end were made in Ghent, Belgium, and transported to the cathedral in pieces. Above them is a large mural depicting St. Louis announcing the Seventh Crusade.

RIGHT: A close-up view of the front of St. Louis Cathedral. Three Roman Catholic churches have stood on this site since 1718. The first was a crude wooden structure in the early days of the colony. This was replaced by a larger brick and timber church begun in 1727 and destroyed by the fire in 1788. The cornerstone of the present church was laid in 1789 and the building was completed in 1794. It was elevated to cathedral status in 1793 and the central tower with the clock and bell was added in 1819. The building was extensively renovated in the 1850s when it took on its current appearance.

Left: Construction of the Presbytere, which was designed to match the Cabildo, was started 1797 and was also funded by Don Andres Almonester y Rojas. The Mansard roof was added in 1847. The building was originally called the Casa Curial (Ecclesiastical House) and was home to Capuchin monks. It later served as a courthouse (from 1847–1911), and is now part of the Louisiana State Museum, housing Mardi Gras exhibits.

Above: Built in 1799, this West Indian-style raised house was originally situated on the banks of Bayou St. John. In the 1960s it was moved to its current location at 1440 Moss Street. The house was purchased in 1810 by James Pitot, who had been the second mayor of New Orleans five years earlier, and is still known as the Pitot House.

Originally named Place d'Armes, the park
before St. Louis Cathedral is now Jackson
Square. The spot where once troops
marched and crimes were punished is a
small but beautiful park, in the center of
which stands a statue of General Jackson.

LEFT: A modern view of the interior of the Pitot House. In 1904 the house was converted into a convent and more recently it has been become a museum that displays antiques and furnishings from the original house.

ABOVE: Known as Madame John's Legacy, this is thought to be the oldest surviving residence in the Mississippi Valley. The building takes its name from the 1873 George Washington Cable novel *Tite Poulette* as Cable used the residence as the basis for the home in his tale. Today, the building houses a museum in which exhibits relate the history of the house and its many residents.

LEFT: This two-storey structure situated at 417 Royal Street was built by Don Vincente Rillieux toward the end of the eighteenth century. By 1804, the building had become the site of the Banque de la Louisiane, the first such financial institution in New Orleans. The intricately designed wrought-iron balcony railing still bears the bank's LB monogram. By 1819, the original Louisiana Bank had outlived its charter and the ground floor of the building was temporarily occupied by the Louisiana State Bank. Since 1954, the building has been occupied by Brennan's Restaurant.

RIGHT: The Napoleon House on Chartres Street consists of two buildings. The first, facing St. Louis Street, is a two-storey structure that was built in 1798; the second, erected in 1814, is the three-storey building with the cupola that is still a local landmark. The two buildings were the home of Mayor Nicholas Girod who once hatched a plan to rescue Napoleon from St. Helena Island and bring him to New Orleans; a plan that had to be abandoned when Napoleon died in 1821. The building is now a bar, but the walls are still lined with Napoleonic memorabilia.

The Louisiana Purchase to the Civil War: 1803–61

The Louisiana Purchase to The Civil War: 1803–61

The Louisiana Purchase added 828,000 square miles of land west of the Mississippi River to the United States. For roughly four cents an acre the Americans had managed to acquire a territory that constitutes twenty-two percent of the present size of the nation and whose natural resources would bring wealth beyond anyone's wildest calculations. New Orleans would be at the hub of this prosperity.

The key to New Orleans success would be its control of the river traffic. Prior to the advent of the steamboats, cargo was transported along the Mississippi on flat-boats that often took several weeks to reach their destination, but the times of these journeys were now dramatically reduced and by the early 1830s around 1,000 boats a year were docking at the bustling port of New Orleans. Foreign imports doubled in just two years between 1831 and 1833.

This huge increase in trade through the city naturally led to a boom period and the antebellum (before the war) years are widely regarded as the golden age of the South and New Orleans in particular. The new wealth was to be reflected in the city itself. Natural gas was introduced around 1830, the Pontchartrain

RIGHT: This 1815 map of New Orleans shows the city gradually expanding beyond the boundaries of its colonial days. The map is framed by drawings of important civic buildings of the time.

PREVIOUS PAGE: This nineteenth century engraving depicts a busy scene on the levee at New Orleans. The advent of steamships would lead to a golden age of prosperity for the city.

RIGHT: This painting shows soldiers in the Place d'Armes raising an American flag and firing a salute during the ceremony in which Louisiana was officially transferred from France to the United States.

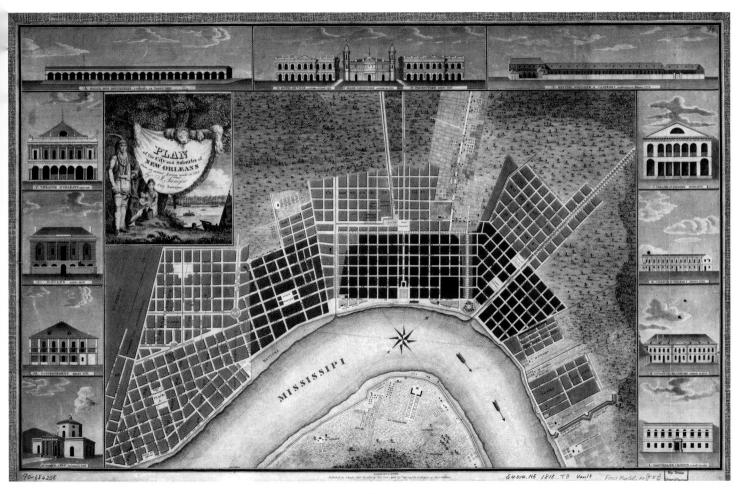

Rail-Road was constructed between 1830 and 1831, and by 1840 there were the beginnings of a public school system in place. In 1837, the first documented Mardi Gras parade was held and 1857 saw the first Mardi Gras parade sponsored by a Krewe.

In 1836, the city was split into three boroughs; the French Quarter and Fauberg Treme comprised the first, Uptown (at that time all the inhabited areas upriver form Canal Street) was the second, and the third was Downtown (the remainder of the city

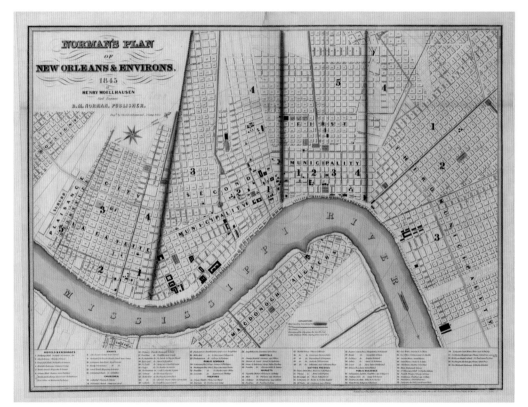

LEFT: Drawn just thirty years after the map on the previous page, in 1845, the environs of the upwardly mobile city had begun to spread out around the bend of the Mississippi River. The emerging town of Algiers, which would become part of New Orleans in 1870, can be seen on the opposite bank of the river.

RIGHT: An exterior view of the Old Absinthe House at the corner of Bourbon Street and Bienville. Built in 1806 to house the importing firm of Pedro Front and Francisco Juncadelia of Barcelona, it gained notoriety, and the name "The Absinthe Room," when Cayetano Ferrer created the "Absinthe House Frappe" here in 1874. The front room still houses a tavern known as Jean Lafitte's Old Absinthe House.

from Esplanade Avenue and downriver). For the next two decades these three boroughs were in effect run as three separate cities.

Biloxi replaced New Orleans as the state capital in 1849, but this had no great negative effect on the city. One of the ironies of the time was that despite having one of the United States largest populations of African-Americans, New Orleans, as a major port, was also one of the chief centers of the slave trade.

Lower Mississippi Plantations

In 1850, over half of America's millionaires lived on plantations located along the Great River Road. Although not sited within the city limits, no visit to New Orleans would be complete without a trip to see some of these magnificent plantations. Not only are they beautiful in their own right but the fortunes of the city were inextricably tied to the trade generated by production at the plantations.

PREVIOUS PAGE: This home on the Destrehan Plantation was originally built for Robert de Logny in 1787 by Charles Pacquet, a free African-American. The house was used by Union troops to house freed slaves during the Civil War.

LEFT: Oak Alley takes its name from the twenty-eight oaks that form a wonderful canopy along the driveway to the striking house shown in this picture. The house and its grounds are so visually stunning that they have been used as a location for several Hollywood movies, including the quintessential New Orleans tale *Interview with the Vampire*, which starred Tom Cruise and Brad Pitt.

RIGHT: The Houmas House was built by Alexandre Latil in 1776 on land that he purchased from the Houmas Indians. In 1858, the house and 10,000 acres of land were sold to the wealthy Irish merchant John Burnside who built up a 20,000 acre sugar plantation.

PREVIOUS PAGE, LEFT: The Nottoway Plantation, shown here, is the largest on this section of the Mississippi. The mansion has sixty-four rooms and covers 53,000 square feet. It was designed by Henry Howard for John Hampden Randolph and built in 1859.

PREVIOUS PAGE, RIGHT: Built in 1856 for Edmond Bozonier Marmillion, the ornate San Francisco House was originally decorated in rich blues, purples, and greens and has been described as the epitome of "Steamboat Gothic." It is thought that due to the enormous cost of renovations undertaken in 1860 the house was nicknamed "Saint Frusquin," from the French *sans fruscins* (without a penny), by Edmond's son Valsin. Over time this was corrupted to "San Francisco."

LEFT: New Orleans won martial laurels in 1815 as the site of the last battle in the war with Great Britain. Despite the Treaty of Ghent having been signed the previous month, the British under General Edward Pakenham launched an attack on the city that was beaten back by the Americans under Major General Andrew Jackson.

LEFT: This fountain is located in the Brulatour Court at 520 Royal Street. The house was built in 1816 for Francois Seignouret, a furniture maker and wine importer from Bordeaux. It is one of the few four-walled courtyards in the French Quarter.

BELOW: The Cat's Meow on Bourbon Street is renowned these days as one of the liveliest bars in the district and was also one of the first in America to try out karaoke. Despite this very modern use it remains an excellent example of the 1820s architecture that is prevalent in the area.

LEFT: This 1821 building, currently an antique shop, once housed the Louisiana State Bank. It was designed by the architect Benjamin Latrobe who was also responsible for the southern wing of the U.S. Capitol.

RIGHT: The Crescent City Billiard Hall at the corner of Canal Street and St. Charles Avenue dates from 1826, though the Italianate façade, designed by Henry Howard, was added in 1875. Since 1950, the upper floor has served as the clubhouse of the Pickwick Club, the public counterpart to the secret Mistic Krewe of Comus that was formed just before the Civil War. It was the first of the New Orleans Mardi Gras Krewes.

Mardi Gras

The most famous party in one of the world's most famous party towns is the New Orleans Mardi Gras, held each year on the day before Ash Wednesday. Since the 1700s, the time between Twelfth Night and Ash Wednesday has been celebrated with extravagant balls held by private groups known as "krewes." Although the balls are mostly private affairs, many of the krewes put on lavish parades featuring flamboyant costumes and ornate floats. It is these colorful parades that revellers from around the world flock to see.

These two pictures, separated by ninety years, show masked characters and elaborate floats during the Rex Parade at the climax of Mardi Gras in 1907 and 1997 respectively. The Krewe of Rex was founded in 1872 by a group of businessmen partly to put on a spectacle to honor the visiting Grand Duke Alexis of Russia during the 1872 carnival season. The Krewe of Rex has since put on more parades in New Orleans than any other organization.

PREVIOUS PAGE: Mardi Gras celebrations in 1910.

FAR LEFT: The King (Rex) of Mardi Gras, usually a prominent local citizen, is chosen each year by the Rex organization. Shown here is business executive Robert Monsted, Jr. who was selected to lead the parade in 2004.

LEFT: Costumed krewe members on floats toss strings of beads, plastic cups, and other favors during a parade along St. Charles Avenue. The purple, green, and gold colors that are prevalent in the costumes and decorations during the carnival season originate in the costume worn by Rex in the 1872 parade. Originally used for a theatrical production of Richard III, the costume consisted of a purple velvet cloak with green rhinestones and a gold scepter and crown.

ABOVE: Actor Elijah Wood reigns as Bacchus 2004 during the Krewe of Bacchus Parade in Uptown New Orleans. Since 1968, the Krewe of Bacchus has invited a guest celebrity each year to reign. Past stars have included Bob Hope, Kirk Douglas, and Charlton Heston.

LEFT: The LaLaurie House at 1140 Royal Street is still viewed with trepidation by some residents of the French Quarter because of its gruesome past and ghostly reputation. It was built in 1832 for the prominent couple Dr. LaLaurie and his wife Delphine who were renowned for their lavish parties. On April 10, 1834, a fire broke out in the property; when neighbors had doused the flames they discovered the horrific remains of a number of tortured slaves as well as grisly looking torture implements. The scene was so sickening that, as word spread, a mob gathered at the house to exact revenge. By then the LaLaurie's had fled and were never seen in New Orleans again, but ever since there have been rumors of ghostly goings on at the property.

RIGHT: Custom House on Canal Street is one of the most impressive Federal-style buildings in the South. Originally designed by Alexander Thompson Wood, who was succeeded by James Dakin, work began on the building in 1847 and was completed in 1881. In the course of its history the building has been a post office, an armory, and a Union prison.

LEFT AND RIGHT: The original church on this site at 724 Camp Street was erected in 1833 to minister to the Irish Catholic population, but was replaced in 1841 by the building that stands here today. This impressive church has a high tower of 185 feet and a stunning Gothic-style interior. The ornate ceiling is an imitation of the one at Exeter Cathedral in England. The building has been declared a National Historic Landmark by the Department of the Interior.

LEFT: The LaBranche Buildings at 700 Royal Street were constructed in 1835 for the sugar planter Jean Baptiste LaBranche and remain a charming example of both the architecture and oak-leaf ironwork of the period.

RIGHT: The Greek Revival-style Old U.S. Mint was built in 1835 by William Strickland and, as its name suggests, operated as a mint until 1909. It was converted into a federal prison in 1931 and was later used by the Coast Guard. In the late 1970s it was converted into the museum that still houses the New Orleans Jazz Collection.

LEFT: Although known as the Le Prete Mansion, this building was, in fact, built in the fall of 1835 by Dr. Joseph Coulon Gardette, a dentist who arrived in New Orleans from Philadelphia during the Spanish Rule. Four years after its completion Gardette sold it to the merchant Jean Baptiste Le Prete for $20,049. The building was taken over by the Citizens Bank in 1870.

RIGHT: Since its dedication in 1842, St. Augustine's church in the Treme neighborhood has been a church for the free African-American citizens of New Orleans, welcoming both free and slave as worshippers. Apart from a short time while its sanctuary was being enlarged in 1925, the church has continued to serve the community to the present day.

LEFT AND BELOW: In 1921, the Pontalba family sold the Lower Pontalba Building and in 1927 it was given to the state museum. Known as the 1850 House, the museum recreates an apartment from the time of its original construction. Seen here are the parlor and kitchen of the 1850 House, decorated with period furniture.

LEFT: The daughter of Don Andres Almonester y Rojas, Baroness Micaela Pontalba, commissioned the building of these block-long apartments in 1848. Occupying the uptown and downtown sides of Jackson Square, they cost over $300,000 to build and were considered to be the finest apartments of their kind at the time.

New Orleans Ironwork

The ironwork that can be seen on the fences and balconies throughout the city, particularly in the French Quarter and the Garden District, contributes greatly to the romantic feel of New Orleans. Hand fashioned wrought iron came first, shaped by German, Irish, and African-American artisans. Cast iron, which is poured into wooden mould and left to set, soon followed.

LEFT: The Pontalba Buildings started the fashion for ironwork in New Orleans. Some of the original patterns were designed by the Baroness's son; this view is from a second storey balcony of the Pontalba Buildings.

RIGHT: Located at 1331 Third Street, the Musson-Bell House is a handsome Italianate villa built in 1853 for the prominent Creole cotton merchant Michel Musson. Both the railings and the balconies provide excellent examples of the intricate ironwork typical of the era.

PREVIOUS PAGE: The balconies throughout the city are frequently adorned with plants and flowers, adding to the charm that they bring to the area. This colorful example is located on Bourbon Street.

LEFT: The cornstalk fence at 915 Royal Street is possibly the most famous of all the ironwork on display in New Orleans. It is similar to the fence at Colonel Short's Villa in the Garden District and was cast at the Philadelphia foundry of Wood & Perot. This Victorian building and its fence are on the National Register of Historic Places. It was once the home of Judge Francois Xavier-Martin, the first Chief Justice of the Louisiana Supreme Court and author of the first history of Louisiana.

RIGHT: Situated at 339–343 Royal Street, this balcony detail is on the Rillieux-Waldhorn House, now the home of Waldhorn Antiques (established 1881). The building was built between 1795 and 1800 for Vincent Rillieux, the great-grandfather of the artist Edgar Degas. The wrought-iron balconies are an excellent example of Spanish colonial workmanship.

New Orleans in 1852, by which time the city was the second biggest port in the United States (after New York). In 1848, the opening of the Illinois & Michigan Canal, far to the north in Chicago meant that for the first time there was a navigable route from New York City to New Orleans via the Great Lakes and Mississippi.

LEFT AND RIGHT: One of the largest urban parks in North America, the original 100 acres of City Park, which once constituted the Allard Plantation, were designated parkland in 1854. Over the next century and a half City Park has grown to 1,500 acres and now boasts a huge variety of attractions from the New Orleans Museum of Art (1911) and New Orleans Botanical Gardens, which date to the 1930s (both pictured) to a golf course, children's carousel, and casino. As an interesting historical footnote, the park was once a notorious site for gentlemen to settle *affaires d'honneur* until duelling was banned in 1890.

ABOVE: The high pressure steamboat *Mayflower*, painted in 1855. The first steamboat arrived in New Orleans in 1812 and over the following decades the boats that have come to symbolize the city dominated the river and helped to build New Orleans' fortune, carrying huge cargoes of cotton from plantations upriver to the busy port in a fraction of the time it had taken sailing vessels. By the time that this illustration was painted around 30,000 steamboats docked annually at New Orleans.

RIGHT: The paddle steamer *Natchez*, which was launched in 1975, is actually the ninth boat to bear the name. One of her predecessors, the fourth *Natchez* famously raced the *Robert E. Lee* down the Mississippi. The riverboat is a much-loved reminder of New Orleans's past and a popular tourist attraction.

LEFT: The only surviving masterpiece of the renowned local architect James Gallier Sr., the Gallier Hall was built between 1845 and 1850 at a cost of $342,000. In 1852 it became the City Hall. Many famous figures, including Jefferson Davis, have lain in state here.

RIGHT: Designed in 1857 by James Gallier's son, James Gallier, Jr., this attractive residence at 1132 Royal Street is now a museum. The building combines elements of Creole architecture with Federal-style windows and doorways. It also contained recent innovations of the time such as a hot-water and a ventilation system.

LEFT AND RIGHT:
The parlor and dining
room at the Gallier
House Museum
furnished in the
opulent style of a
wealthy antebellum
owner.

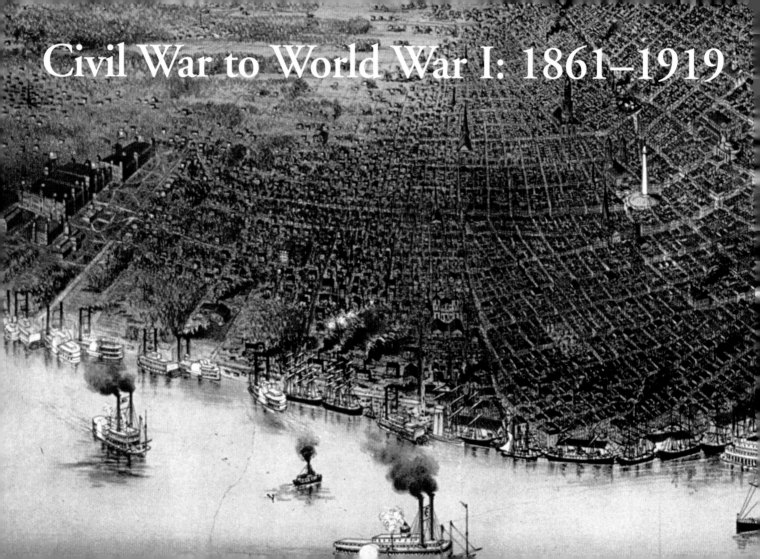

Civil War to World War I: 1861–1919

Civil War to World War I: 1861–1919

The advent of the Civil War signaled a downturn in fortunes for New Orleans. With the destruction of the upriver plantations, the source of much of the city's wealth was gone and combined with an economic shift to the cities of the northeast this led to troubled times. New Orleans was also beset by problems caused by racial tensions following the war. Slaves were freed but, especially in the South, existed in a legal limbo. On July 30, 1866, there was a violent street riot when a crowd laid siege to the Mechanics Hall in downtown New Orleans where a new state constitution designed to extend full rights to black men was being drafted. The ensuing fighting saw the deaths of thirty-seven men and the wounding of a further 136. In 1874, there was a pitched battle between the White League and the Republican metropolitan police that forced the temporary exile of the incumbent government.

Despite this upheaval, the city continued to expand and improve. In the 1890s the majority of the New Orleans public transport system was electrified, having previously relied primarily on mule-drawn streetcars and a few steam locomotives. In 1896, the city's first public library, The New Orleans Public Library, was opened after Mayor John Fitzpatrick amalgamated the city's existing library resources.

However, crime and corruption continued to blight the city and in an attempt to marginalize and contain the majority of illegal activity, Alderman Sidney Story proposed a bill in 1897 to legalize prostitution in a specific area of the city. This thirty-eight-block area, bordered by Iberville, Basin, Robertson, and St. Louis streets became known as "Storyville" and is frequently credited as the birthplace of modern jazz music as many early musicians began plying their trade in the bordellos of the area.

Storyville survived until it was closed down by the Department of the Navy on October 2, 1917, due to fears that it would prove too much of a distraction for sailors departing for World War I. The mayor at the time, Martin Behrman, opposed the move and was famously quoted as saying "You can make it illegal, but you can't make it unpopular."

PREVIOUS PAGE: This color illustration from 1885 shows that despite the economic hardship that followed the Civil War, New Orleans remained a busy port for traffic along the Mississippi.

RIGHT: Designed by Henry Howard and built for the Virginia tobacco merchant Walter Robinson between 1859 and 1865, this house is one of the largest and most majestic in the Garden District. It was one of the first houses in the city to have indoor plumbing.

LEFT: This Victorian Renaissance Revival-style plantation house was built around 1870 for the Civil War diarist Felix Pierre Poche. Poche was also a Democratic Party leader and one of the founders of the American Bar Association.

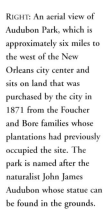

RIGHT: An aerial view of Audubon Park, which is approximately six miles to the west of the New Orleans city center and sits on land that was purchased by the city in 1871 from the Foucher and Bore families whose plantations had previously occupied the site. The park is named after the naturalist John James Audubon whose statue can be found in the grounds.

The Cities of the Dead

In the early days of the colony, New Orleans earned the nickname "the Wet Grave" because, due to the high water table, coffins placed in the ground would often float up to the surface. To avoid this, the citizens began to bury their dead above ground in the elaborate cemeteries that have since become an integral part of the city's image.

LEFT: This aerial view of Metarie Cemetery, built in 1872 and located on the grounds of a former horse-racing track, demonstrates how the cemeteries earned their name as the "Cities of the Dead." Laid out in a similar grid pattern to New Orleans itself, from this perspective the cemeteries resemble nothing more than miniature cities.

RIGHT: This beautiful, ornate gateway is the entrance to one of the more unique cemeteries in New Orleans, St. Roch's. During 1867, New Orleans was in the grip of a terrible epidemic of yellow fever. The Reverend Peter Thevis prayed to St. Roch, a medieval saint who had tended to plague victims. Following his prayers the Rev. Thevis's congregation was spared and he oversaw the creation of the cemetery and its famous chapel.

LEFT: The tomb of Marie Laveau in St. Louis No. 1 Cemetery. Marie Laveau was the most famous voodoo priestess to live in in the city (there is a voodoo shop on Bourbon Street named in her honor). Her tomb continues to attract visitors who draw three crosses (XXX), as can be seen in the picture, on its side, hoping that her spirit will grant them a wish.

RIGHT: Tombs and a statue in the St. Louis No.3 Cemetery on Esplanade Avenue. Established in 1854, this is one of the most elegant cemeteries in the city and there is still a waiting list for burial spaces.

OVER PAGE: The Jefferson Fire Company No.22 tomb is located in the St. Louis No.1 Cemetery. The area was originally part of the Livaudais plantation in the City of Lafayette and has been used for burials since 1824. The cemetery was laid out by Benjamin Buisson. When New Orleans annexed Lafayette in 1852, the graveyard became the city cemetery, the first planned cemetery in New Orleans.

Taken around 1880, this photograph shows the French Market in the French Quarter. The area's use as a market predates European settlement—Choctaw Indians once used the natural levee here as a trading point. The market's name belies the rich mixture of nationalities who have sold their wares here throughout New Orleans' history. At the time that the photo was taken, many market stalls were in the hands of Italian traders.

This contemporary lithograph shows the Horticultural Hall at the 1884 World's Industrial and Cotton Centennial Exposition that was held in Audubon Park. The build up to the Exposition had been plagued by corruption and scandal, most notably the disappearance of Fair Director Edward A. Burke to Brazil with over one and a half million dollars of the fair treasury. The main building at the exposition covered 130,000 square meters. As well as the Horticultural Hall there was also a large U.S.A. Government & State Exhibits Hall, an observation tower with electric elevators, and working examples of various experimental designs of electric streetcars.

A view down Canal Street in 1870 showing a busy city street full of life. The monument to Henry Clay that can be seen in the middle of the street had to be redesigned dramatically because the large round base of the monument caused an obstruction to streetcars. Nevertheless, the statue continued to cause traffic problems and in 1901 it was relocated to Lafayette Park, where it remains today.

LEFT: The Commanders Palace Restaurant has been at 1403 Washington Avenue since 1880. When it was first opened by Emile Commander it was the only restaurant regularly patronized by the distinguished families of the surrounding Garden District. During the 1920s it developed a more racy reputation and was frequented by riverboat captains and couples heading for an illicit rendezvous in the private dining room upstairs.

RIGHT: The first statue in the United States to honor a woman is believed to be that of Margaret Haughery shown here. Sculpted in 1884, by Alexander Doyle, it is located at the intersection of Prytania and Camp streets. As an Irish immigrant who was orphaned at the age of nine, Margaret lost her husband, Charles Haughery, and newborn baby to the yellow fever epidemic of 1835. Despite these setbacks she went on to become a hugely respected local businesswoman and philanthropist and was a great benefactor of widows and orphans in the area.

LEFT: The Jax Brewery at 600 Decatur Street was the brewing and bottling plant for Jax Beer from 1890 through to the mid 1970s. Today, the building is a shopping area that also contains a free museum devoted to the brewery.

ABOVE: The Café Du Monde was established in 1862 on Decatur Street and continues to operate as a coffee house today. During the mid-nineteenth century there were many coffee houses in the French Quarter. In fact, the trade in the bean was one of the factors that helped New Orleans recover from the economic destabilization caused by the Civil War.

Canal Street is one of New Orleans most famous thoroughfares and the link between the French Quarter and the American Sector. It gained its name from a canal that was proposed, to join the Mississippi to the Basin Canal, but never built. Instead Canal Street became famous for the streetcars that plied their routes along its length.

LEFT: This baroque building, constructed out of Georgia marble, at 400 Royal street looks a little out of place in the French Quarter. Indeed, an entire block of old Creole homes and business buildings was knocked down to make way for it. It was originally home to the parish and state courts and has also housed the Louisiana Wildlife Museum.

BELOW: This picture from 1910 shows ships of the United Fruit Company docked at New Orleans. The shipping trade continued to play an important part in the economy of the city.

ABOVE: Work began on the New Orleans Museum of Art in 1910 when sugar broker Isaac Delgado offered the city $150,000 to build a "temple of art for rich and poor alike" in City Park. The Beaux Arts-style museum was opened in 1911 by which time Delgado was, unfortunately, too ill to attend the ceremony.

ABOVE: The spectacular interior of Delgado Great Hall at the New Orleans Museum of Art measures 25,000 square feet. On his death, only a few weeks following the opening of the museum, Delgado bequeathed an art collection gathered by his late aunt.

A modern view of the riverfront shows Jackson Square and the historic French Quarter (right) towered over by the modern skyscrapers of the Central Business District (left).

World War I to the Present: 1920–Today

World War I to the Present: 1920–Today

Following World War I, New Orleans began to slowly rebuild its fortunes. In 1923, the Industrial Canal was opened to provide a direct shipping link between the Mississippi River and Lake Pontchartrain. Also during the 1920s an attempt was made to modernize the look of the city by removing many of the original cast-iron balconies along Canal Street in the heart of the Central Business District. When the city attempted to rejuvenate its economy through tourism in the late twentieth century both this and a decision taken in the 1960s to replace the Canal Streetcar Line with buses would come to be viewed as short-sighted mistakes.

The economy of New Orleans was hit hard by the Depression of the late 1920s and early 1930s, the extent of the problem was such that in 1933 eleven percent of the eligible population were on welfare and five New Orleans banks went bust.

Rebuilding of both the economy and civic building programmes began in 1933 with money from the New Deal. By the latter half the twentieth century the Central Business District was beginning to take on the look of a truly modern city, with the building of high-rise offices and hotels such as the World Trade Center and Place St. Charles.

By the 1980s a degree of prosperity had returned to New Orleans and this was to continue with the development of the tourist industry through the 1990s.

The Higgins Plant, seen here in 1942, played a large part of the economic regeneration that came to the shipyards of New Orleans during World War II.

Carondelet Street looking south; on the right, the Federal Reserve Bank, the Maritime Building, the Marine Building, the New Orleans Cotton Exchange, and the Hibernian Bank Building.

LEFT AND RIGHT: Views of the Longue Vue house and gardens. The cotton broker Edgar Stern and his wife, heiress to the Sears fortune, Edith Rosenwald established the Longue Vue estate between 1939 and 1942. The interior of the house is decorated with beautiful fine art and antiques while the gardens are adorned with twenty-three fountains created by Ellen Biddle and are wonderful examples of landscape gardening, the largest on the estate being modelled on the fourteenth century Alhambra gardens in Spain.

Although in recent times City Hall has become run down and has been the source of many problems for the city's administration, when it was unveiled in 1957 it was viewed as a perfect example of the post World War II modernist movement in public facilities. Designed by two leading local architectural firms, Goldstein, Parham, and Labouisse and Favrot, Reed, Mathes, and Bergman it was the centerpiece of a modern development that also included $16,000,000 Union Passenger Terminal.

The first of the two bridges, the Crescent City
Connection Bridge (on the right) was opened in 1958
and led to suburban development of the West Bank area
of the city. In 1988, the second bridge was opened and
the first closed down in sections for repair. Prior to
Hurricane Katrina, the Crescent City Connection
ranked as the fifth most traveled toll bridge in the
United States, with the annual traffic volume exceeding
sixty-three million.

LEFT: The John Hancock building was designed in the early 1960s by Skidmore, Owings, and Merrill. It is notable for the sculpture that can be seen in the foreground designed by Isamu Noguchi.

RIGHT: Seen here at the right, in the foreground, the World Trade Center was designed by Edward Durrell Stone in the early 1960s. It was originally called the International Trade Mart and along with Plaza Tower was one of the first 1960s-era high-rise buildings to tower above the New Orleans skyline until the building boom of the 1980s saw the construction of a number of high-rise hotels and offices along Canal Street.

LEFT: Plaza Tower, now called Crescent City Tower, was designed by Leonard Spangenberg, a student of the famed architect Frank Lloyd Wright, and completed in 1968. It was the tallest building in Louisiana until 1972 when it was surpassed by One Shell Square.

RIGHT: Located at 701 Poydras Street, One Shell Square stands 697 feet tall. The building was constructed using a double-tube system, consisting of a steel core and a concrete perimeter with the exterior clad in limestone and bronze glass. One Shell Square remains the tallest building in both New Orleans and Louisiana.

LEFT AND RIGHT: The New Orleans Historic Voodoo Museum first opened its mystical doors in 1972 and became an immediate hit with tourists. The museum is a witness to this unique culture, which took root in the heady racial and religious mix of early New Orleans and celebrates the history of the religion from its origins in slave culture brought over from the West Indies. On display are items that once belonged to famous voodoo practitioner Marie Laveau as well as shrines and supposedly magical objects.

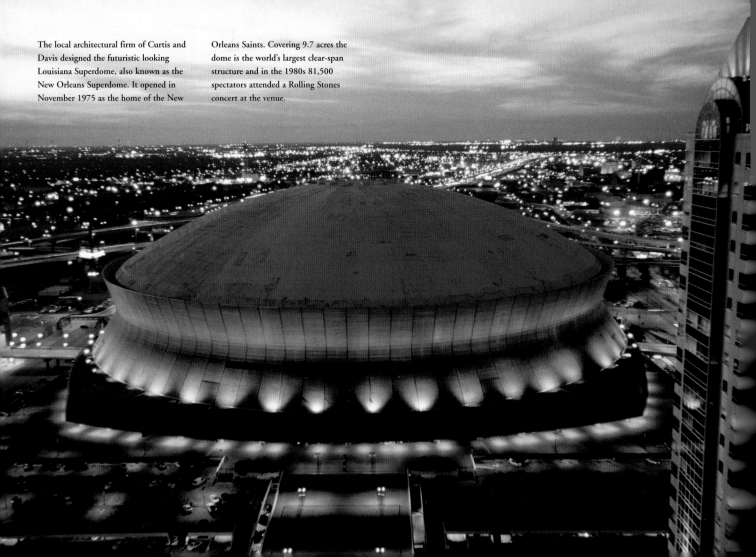

The local architectural firm of Curtis and Davis designed the futuristic looking Louisiana Superdome, also known as the New Orleans Superdome. It opened in November 1975 as the home of the New Orleans Saints. Covering 9.7 acres the dome is the world's largest clear-span structure and in the 1980s 81,500 spectators attended a Rolling Stones concert at the venue.

The fountain that stands in the Spanish Plaza was a gift to New Orleans from Spain. The project was originally proposed by the then Consul General of Spain, Jose Luis Aparicio y Aparicio. Two tiles on the fountain commemorate the gift in English and Spanish, the English version reads thus: "Spain dedicated this plaza to the City of New Orleans in remembrance of their common historical past and as a pledge of fraternity in the future. 1976 AD. Bicentennial Year of the United States. Renovated and Rededicated in the Year 2001 AD. Thanks to the generosity of the Province of Castellon, Spain."

LEFT: Place St. Charles (right) and One Shell Square (left) seen towering above the Central Business District of the French Quarter. Built on the site of the historic St. Charles Hotel, Place St. Charles was completed in 1984. Despite not being as tall as One Shell Square this building has the greatest number of over-ground floors of any New Orleans high-rise.

RIGHT: Part of the redevelopment of the area, the Aquarium of the Americas opened on the riverfront in 1990 and features marine life predominantly from the waters around New Orleans, from the Mississippi and the swamps to the Gulf of Mexico and the Caribbean.

LEFT: The aquatic theme is continued in Woldenberg Riverfront Park, adjacent to the Aquarium of the Americas, with this stainless steel sculpture by the local artist John Scott. Entitled "Ocean Song" the work depicts the gentle motion of the ocean and coupled with the viewer's reflection in the polished surfaces, symbolizes their connection to the sea.

RIGHT: Harrah's Casino was opened in 1999. Situated close to the riverfront, at 601 Poydras Street, it occupies 100,000 square feet. Inside it contains a vast ballroom and five courts, all with a New Orleans theme.

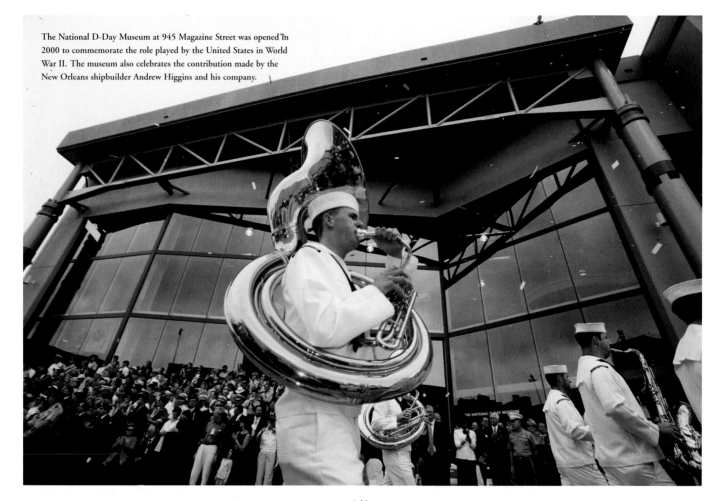

The National D-Day Museum at 945 Magazine Street was opened in 2000 to commemorate the role played by the United States in World War II. The museum also celebrates the contribution made by the New Orleans shipbuilder Andrew Higgins and his company.

In the second half of the twentieth century New Orleans became one of the United States' premier tourist destinations. While striving to modernize, the city took care to preserve, and recreate, its heritage. Companies such as the Delta Queen Steamboat Company operate river cruises on lavishly appointed new riverboats— such as the *Mississippi Queen* shown here—that offer all the atmosphere of a nineteenth century voyage, but with modern conveniences.

The modern skyline of New Orleans taken shortly before Hurricane Katrina struck.

Hurricane Katrina and Beyond

August 29, 2005, is a date that will be indelibly linked with New Orleans and Hurricane Katrina. The storm, which was one of the devastating natural disasters in United States history, was also the most costly hurricane ever to hit the country.

Hurricane Katrina started life on August 23, out in the Atlantic. During the evening of Thursday, August 25, Katrina hit densely populated areas of southeast Florida with punishing winds of over seventy-five miles-per-hour and torrential rain, leaving at least two people dead and over 1,000,000 without electricity. The hurricane then headed west into the Gulf of Mexico. Once in the gulf it turned north and at 07.00 on Monday, August 29, Katrina made landfall on the Louisiana coast between Grand Isle and the mouth of the Mississippi River. By 11.00 Katrina had made another landfall near the Louisiana-Mississippi state line with winds roaring at up to 125 mph. By the end of the day the storm had claimed lives and destroyed property in Louisiana, Mississippi, and Alabama. The following morning saw New Orleans in a state of chaos with no power, no drinking water, diminishing food supplies, fires, and widespread looting. The authorities were forced to start evacuating the thousands of people in city shelters when efforts to limit the flooding were unsuccessful. By August 31, eighty percent of New Orleans was flooded with some parts of the city under up to twenty feet of water. Over eighty percent of the city's residents had evacuated. By August 2006, it was estimated that there were still 200,000 displaced persons who had not been able to return.

Although a visitor to New Orleans today will find the French Quarter and the Garden District unchanged (indeed in these tourist areas there isn't even a hint of the devastation that hurricane Katrina wrought) the reconstruction of other areas of the city is a slow and painful process. Tourists continue to flock to "The Big Easy," pouring badly needed money into the city's economy, but it is impossible to place a value on the cost to those whose lives were affected by this tragedy and it will be a long time before New Orleans and its residents can make anything resembling a full recovery from the events of that fateful day.

The New Orleans skyline as seen on September 16, 2005, after power had been restored to the downtown area following Hurricane Katrina.

These two satellite images from the Advanced Spaceborne Thermal Emission and Reflection Radiometer on NASA's *Terra* satellite show New Orleans before and after Hurricane Katrina struck. The image above was acquired in April and September 2000, and the image on the right was acquired September 13, 2005. The flooded parts of the city appear dark blue, such as the golf course in the northeast corner, where there is standing water. Areas that have dried out appear light blue grey, such as the city park in the left middle. On the left side of the image, the failed Seventeenth Street Canal marks a sharp boundary between flooded city to the east, and dry land to the west.

Water from a levee along the Inner Harbor Navigational Canal pouring into the city after
the structure broke under the force of Hurricane Katrina.

ABOVE: An aerial photograph of the damage taken on Tuesday August 30, 2005. This view is taken looking east toward downtown.

OVER PAGE: Water surrounds homes in this residential area just east of downtown.

149

LEFT: A New Orleans fireman helping to evacuate a man from flood waters as a home burns in the Seventh Ward. Surrounded by water, but with no water service available fire fighters had to wait for tanker trucks of water to arrive and hope that the fires did not spread.

ABOVE: A view of Canal Street, flooded in the aftermath of Hurricane Katrina. New Orleans had been struck by hurricanes in the past, as far back as 1722 when on September 12, over thirty-four buildings were destroyed in the fledgling city. However, none of the previous hurricanes had caused anything like the catastrophic destruction wrought by Katrina.

An aerial view of flooded areas of the city with the New Orleans Arena and Louisiana Superdome prominent in the center of the picture. Although it had provided a refuge for some people, the Superdome had sustained significant damage. The waterproof membrane covering the dome had been effectively peeled off and two sections of the roof were compromised. On August 30, Louisiana Governor Kathleen Banco ordered the complete evacuation of the Superdome.

Side streets off of St. Claude Street in the Ninth Ward of New Orleans shown on September 7, 2005. Floodwaters were thick with sewage-related bacteria at least ten times higher than acceptable safety limits.

LEFT: A waiter serves up hot beignets and coffee to patrons at Café Du Monde on November 17, 2005. Two and half months after Hurricane Katrina tore through New Orleans local businesses had begun re-open.

RIGHT: Residents of the fifth ward watching the Zulu second line parade during Mardis Gras 2006, six months after Hurricane Katrina. New Orleans was still empty in the lower Ninth Ward and St. Bernard's Parish, but many of the city's residents came back to participate and celebrate.